武満 徹

アルト・フルートとギターのための

海へ

TORU TAKEMITSU
TOWARD THE SEA

for alto flute and guitar

SJ 1007

TOWARD THE SEA
海へ
for Alto flute and Guitar

Toru Takemitsu
武満 徹

1. The Night
夜

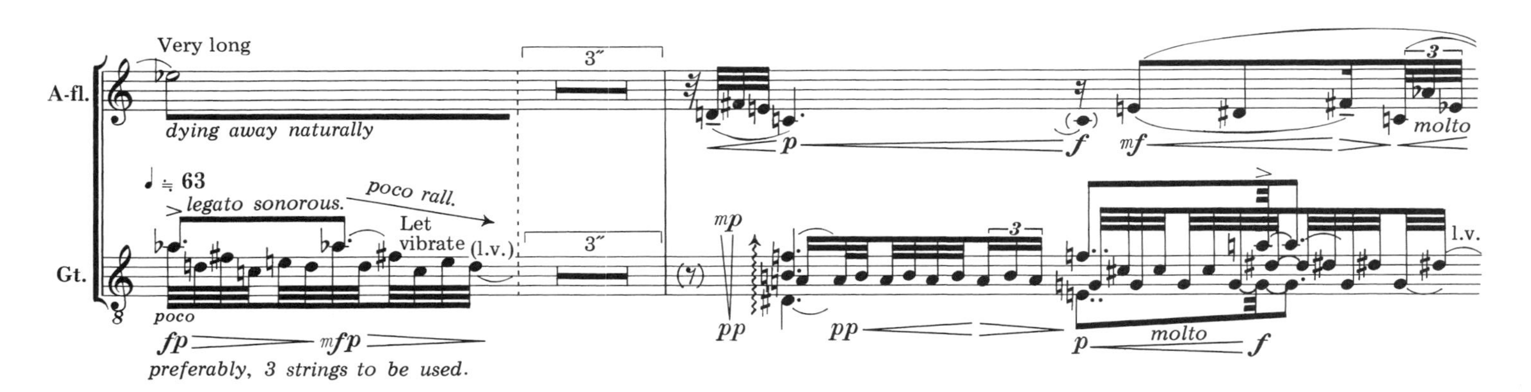

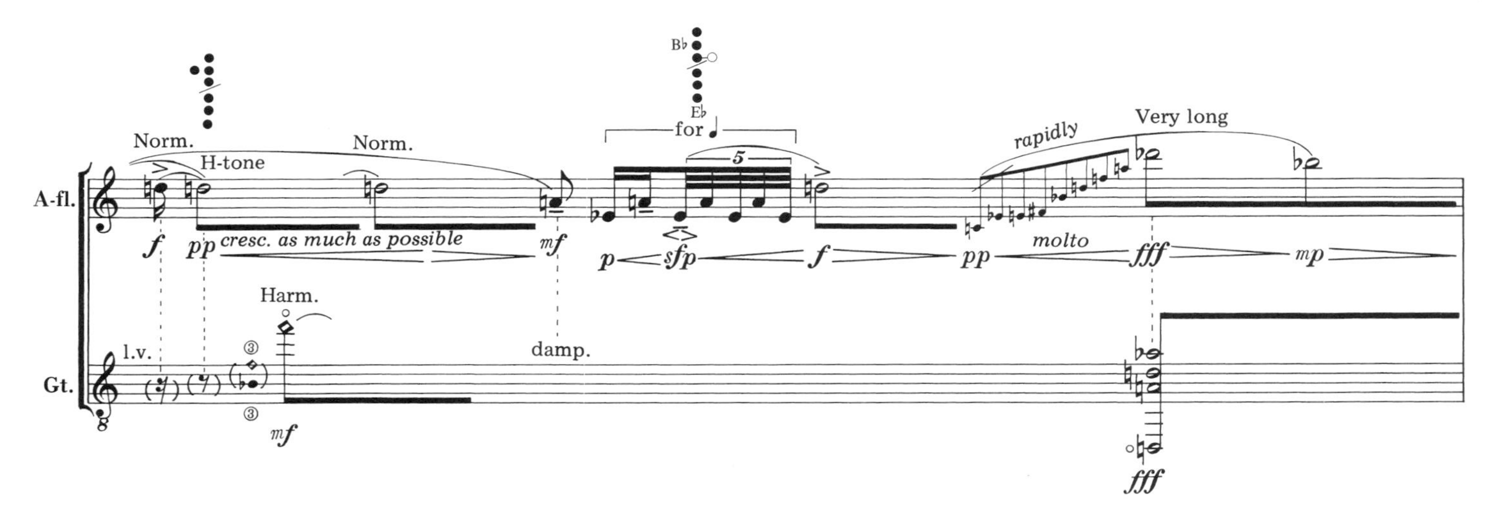

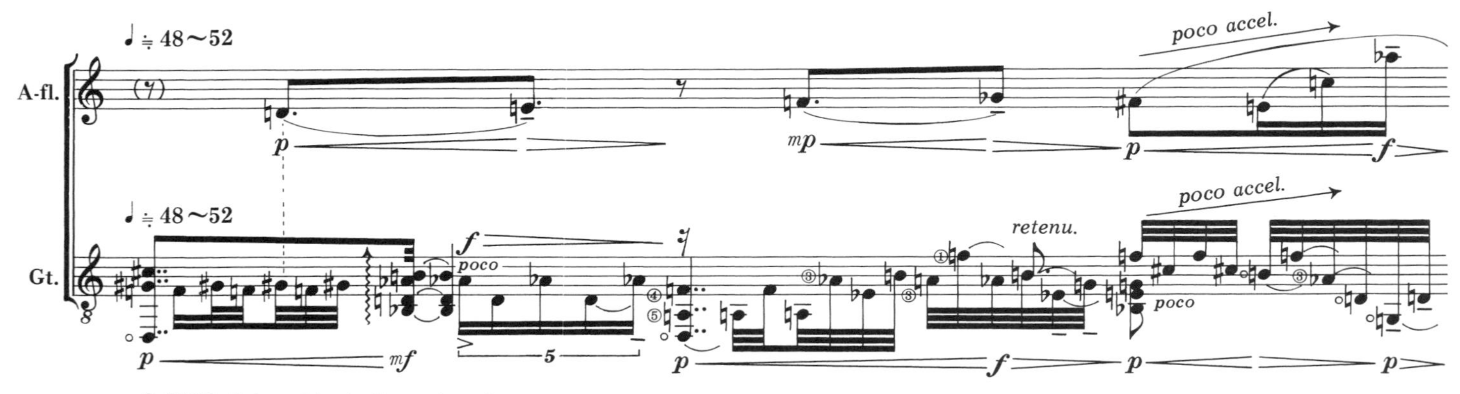

アルト・フルートとギターのための《海へ》の第1部〈夜〉は、ロバート・エイトケンとレオ・ブローウェルによって、1981年2月トロントにおいて初演された。
全3部を通しての初演は、1981年5月31日東京で、小泉浩、佐藤紀雄によっておこなわれた。
この4人の奏者たちの協力、とくに技術的な助言をしてくれた小泉浩と佐藤紀雄に感謝する。

演奏時間——12分

The Night, the first piece of this three-part work *Toward the Sea,* was given its world premiere in Toronto by Robert Aitken and Leo Brouwer n February, 1981.
The three parts were first performed in thei- entirety on May 31, 1981 by Hiroshi Koizumi and Norio Sato in Tokyo.
The composer is most grateful to these four performers for their collaboration, especially for the technical advice of Hiroshi Koizumi and No-io Sato.

Duration: 12 minutes

SYMBOLS AND ABBREVIATIONS:

⌈•⌉	Short fermata
○	open
●	close
●——○ ○——●	alternate changes close (open) and open (close) rapidly
tr.	triller
	should be played long as *senza misura*
l.v.	let vibrate
S.P.	sul ponticello (near the bridge)
ord.	ordinary playing

CHART OF FINGERING NUMBERS:

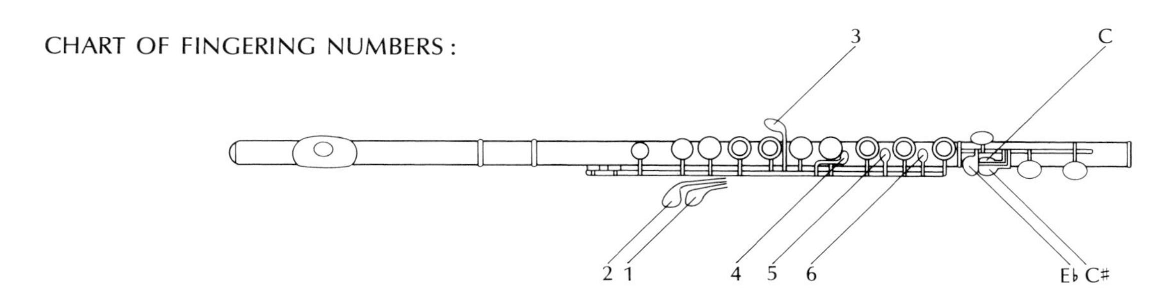

Accidentals apply only to each note.

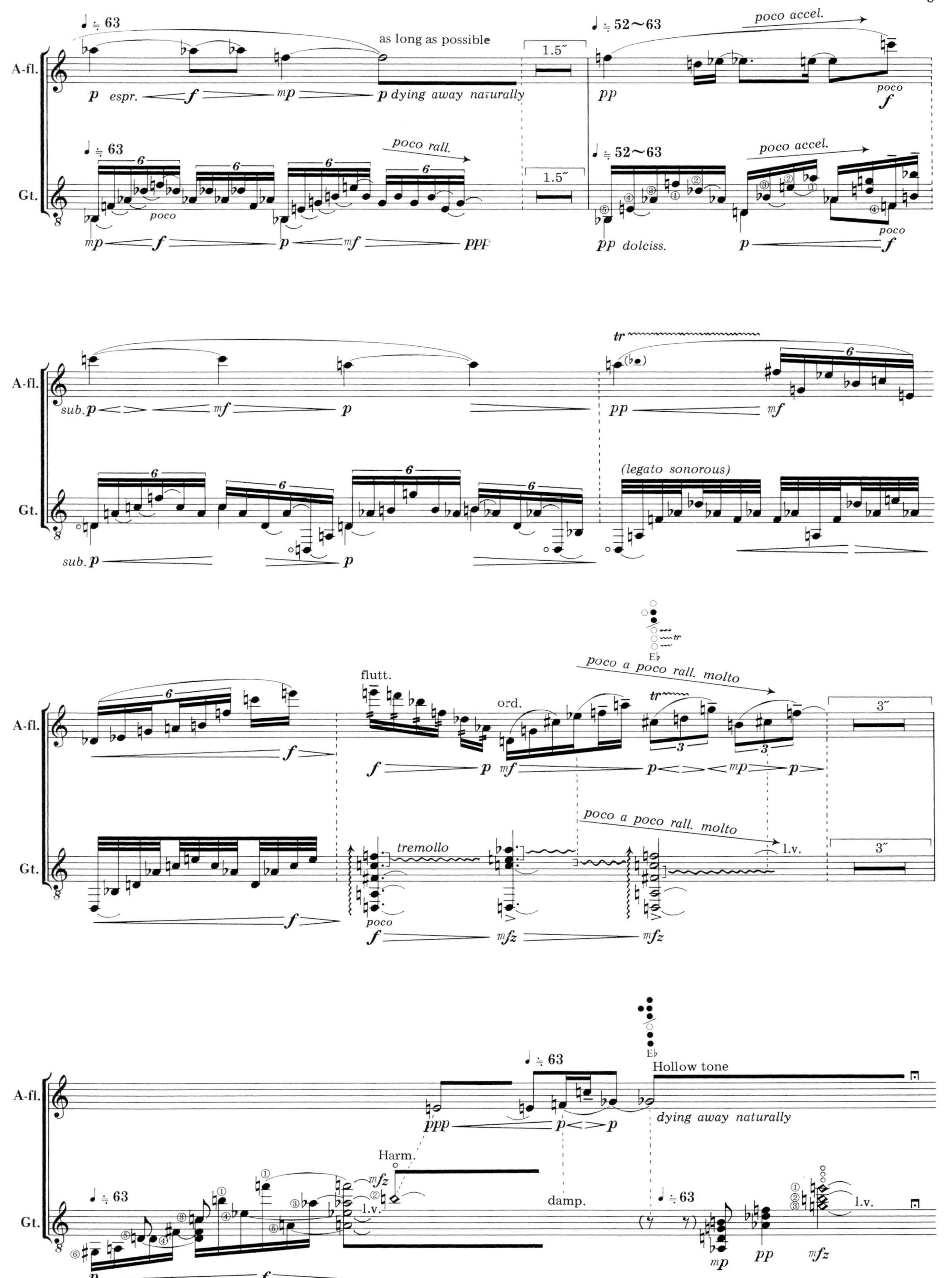
A-fl.
Gt.
♩ ≒ 63
as long as possible
p espr. f mp p dying away naturally
1.5″
♩ ≒ 52〜63
poco accel.
pp poco f
poco rall.
poco
mp f p mf ppp
pp dolciss. p poco f
sub. p mf p
tr
pp mf
(legato sonorous)
sub. p p
f
flutt.
ord.
poco a poco rall. molto
E♭
f p mf p mp p
tremollo
l.v.
3″
poco f mfz mfz
Hollow tone
dying away naturally
ppp p p
Harm.
mfz
l.v.
damp.
p f
mp pp mfz

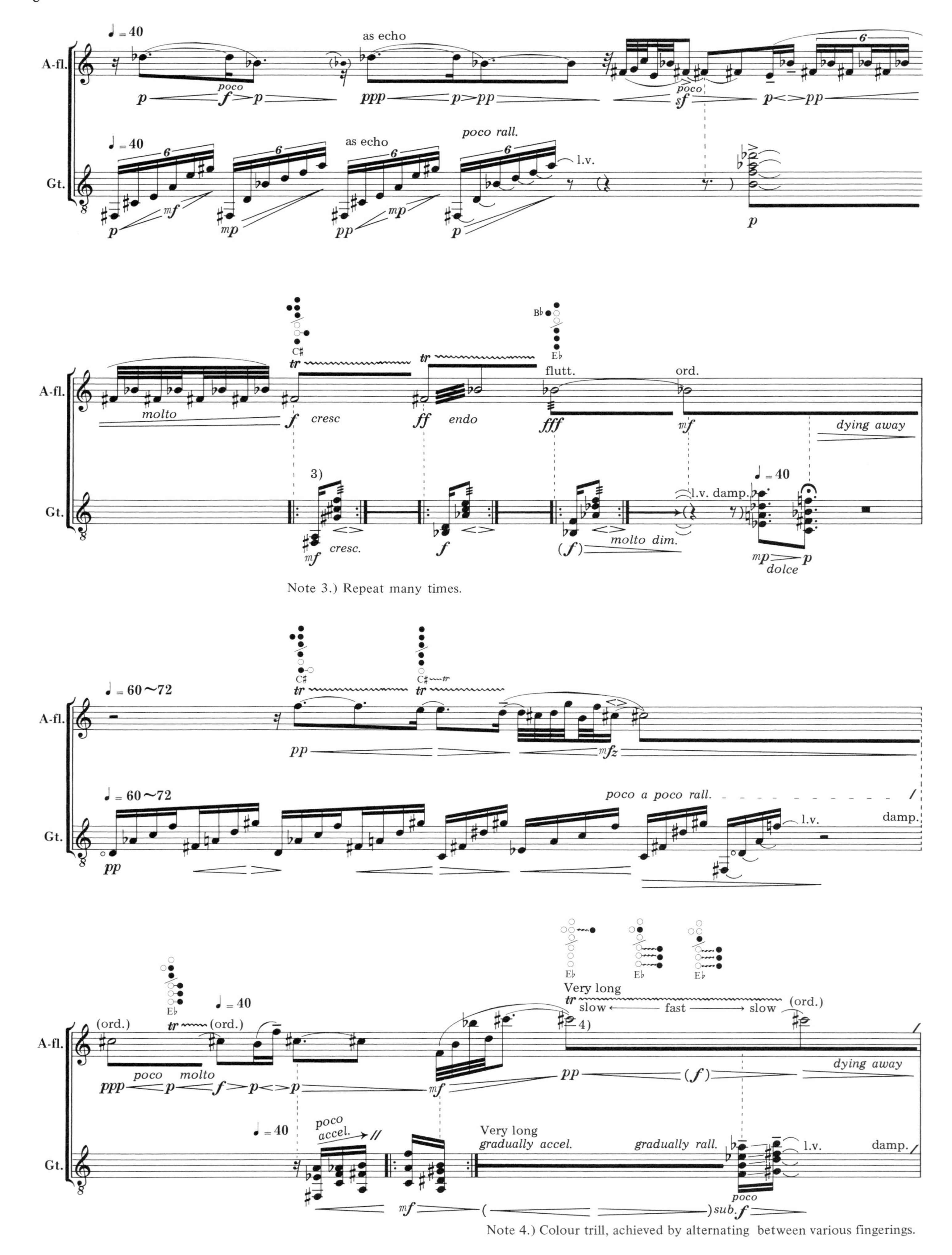

Note 3.) Repeat many times.

Note 4.) Colour trill, achieved by alternating between various fingerings.

2. Moby Dick

白 鯨

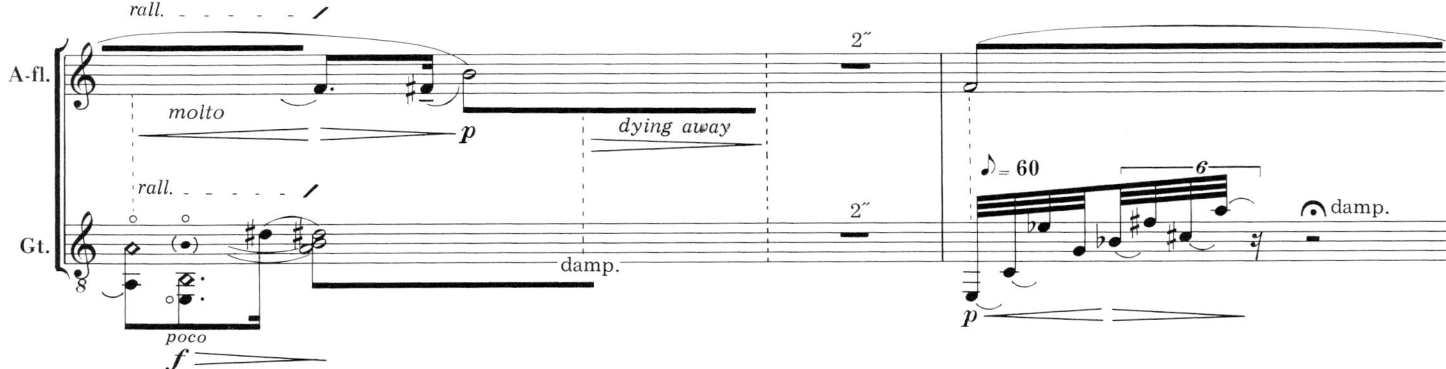

Note 1.) Play ad lib. as tremolo. ex. 

Note 2.)
Gradually bring in the first overtone until both tones are sounding.

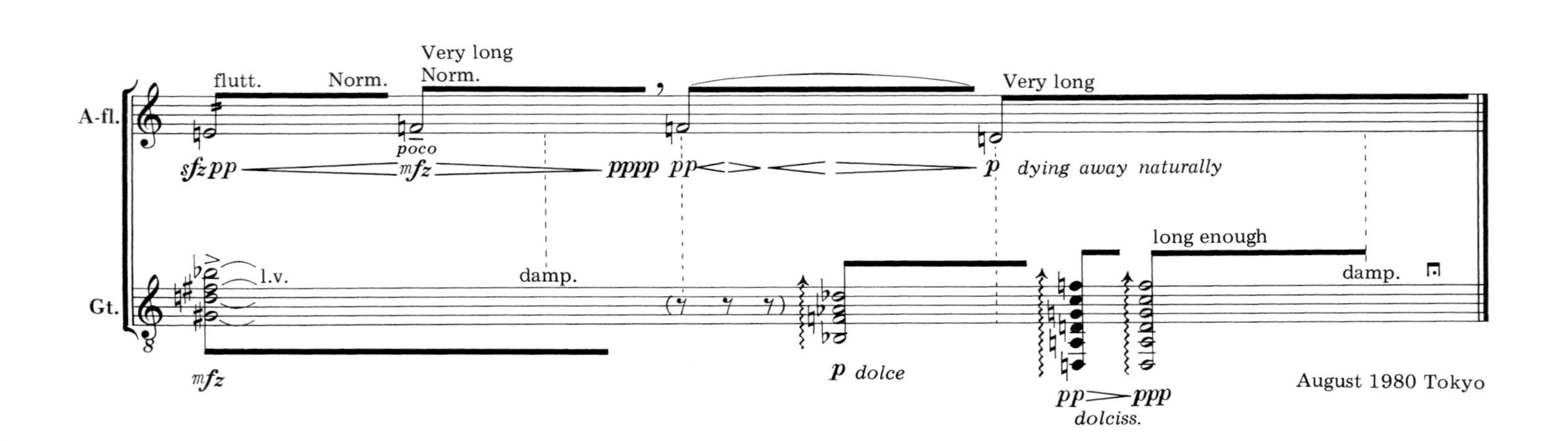

August 1980 Tokyo

3. Cape Cod
鱈岬

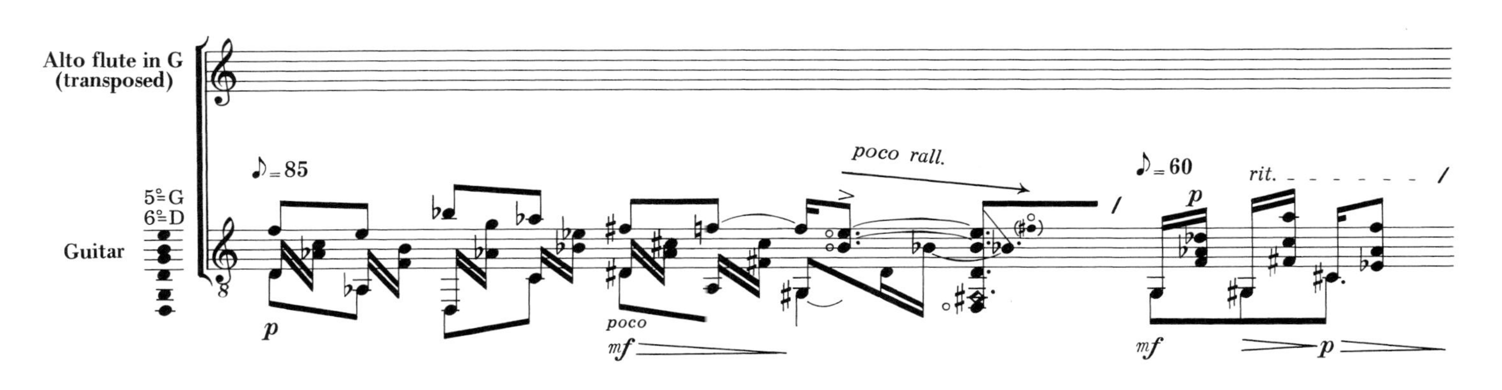

Alto flute in G (transposed)
Guitar
5º=G
6º=D
♪=85
poco rall.
♪=60
rit.
p
poco
mf
mf
p

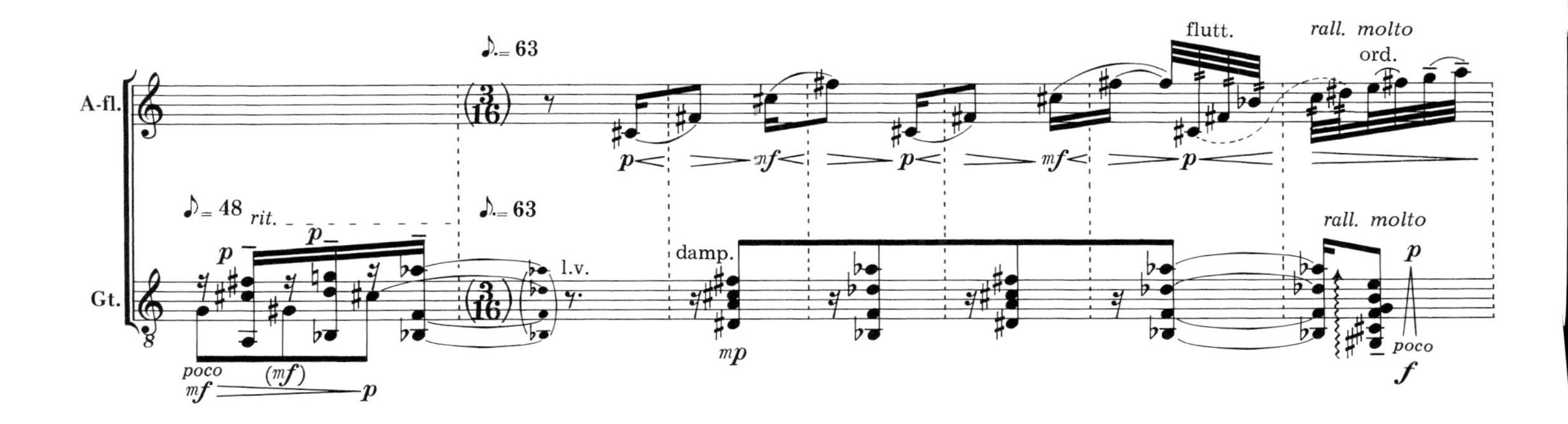

A-fl.
Gt.
♪.=63
flutt.
rall. molto
ord.
p
mf
p
mf
p
♪=48
rit.
p
♪.=63
l.v.
damp.
rall. molto
p
poco
mf
(mf)
mp
poco
f

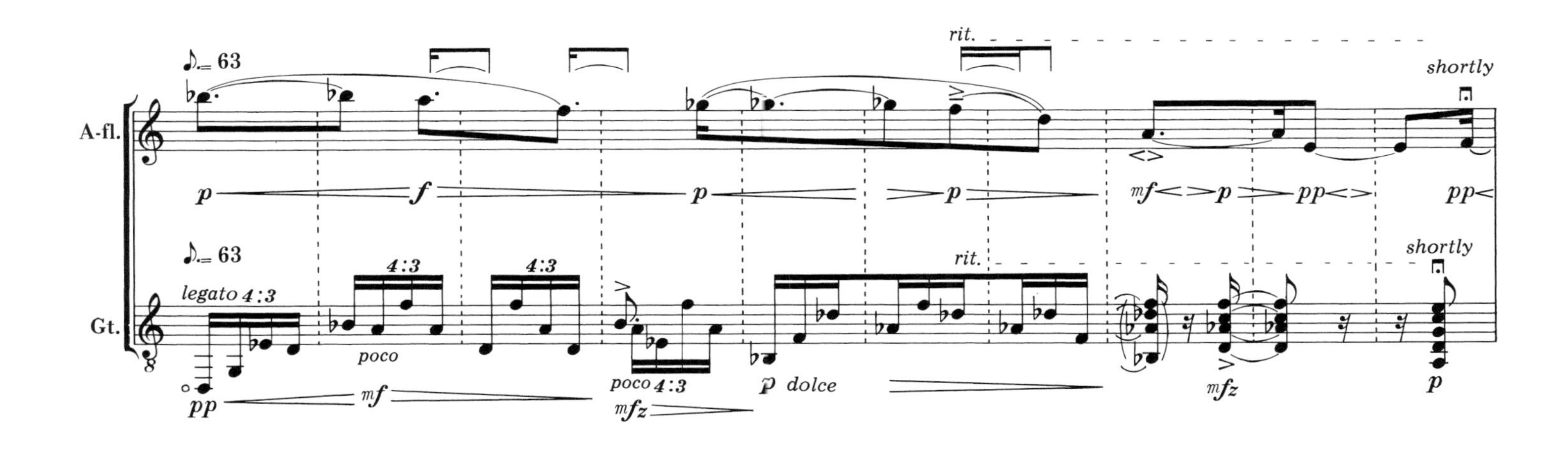

A-fl.
Gt.
♪.=63
rit.
shortly
p
f
p
p
mf
p
pp
pp
legato
4:3
poco
poco
mfz
p dolce
rit.
mfz
shortly
p
pp
mf

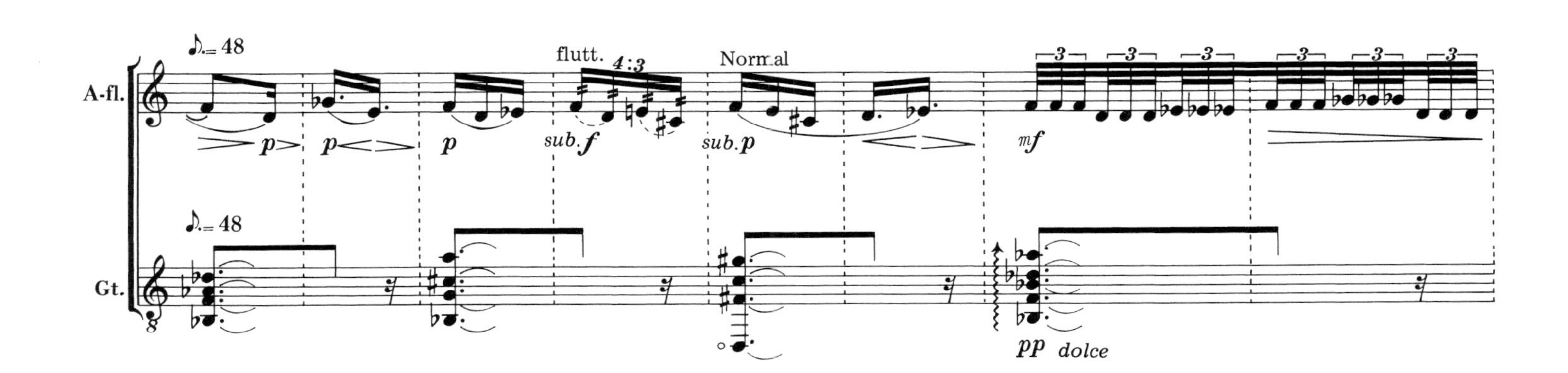

A-fl.
Gt.
♪.=48
flutt.
4:3
Normal
p
p
p
sub. f
sub. p
mf
pp dolce

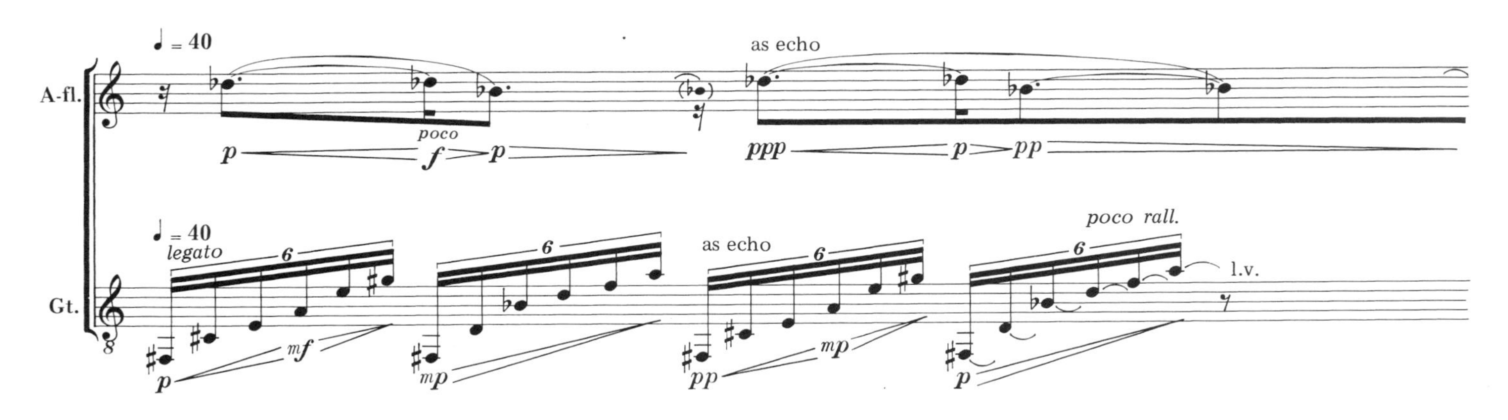
♩ = 40
A-fl.
poco
p f p
as echo
ppp p pp
♩ = 40
legato
6
p mf
mp
as echo
pp mp
poco rall.
l.v.
p
Gt.

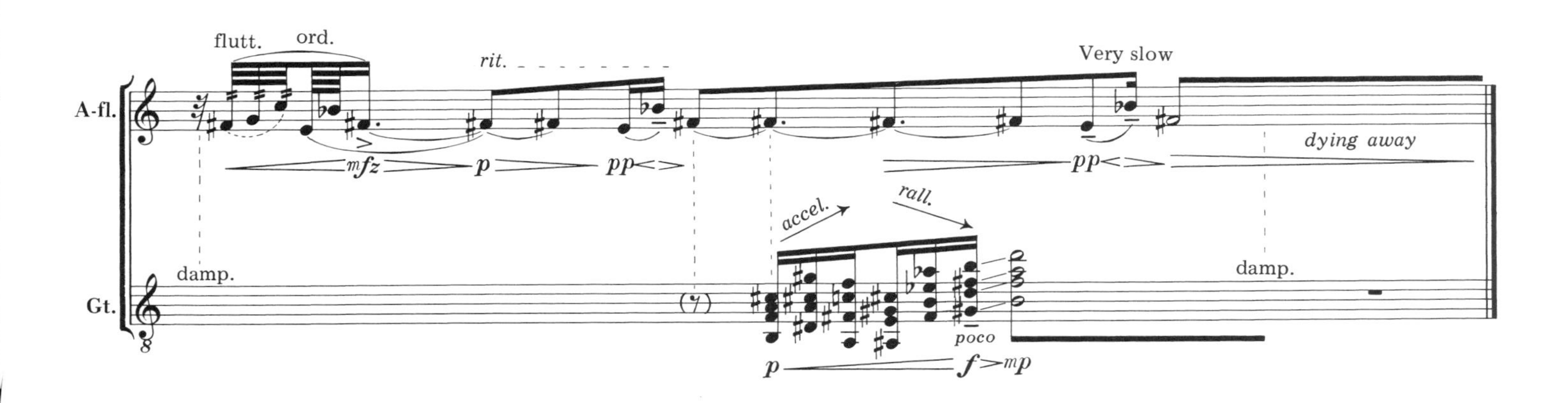
flutt.
ord.
A-fl.
rit.
mfz p pp
Very slow
pp
dying away
accel.
rall.
damp.
Gt.
poco
p f mp
damp.

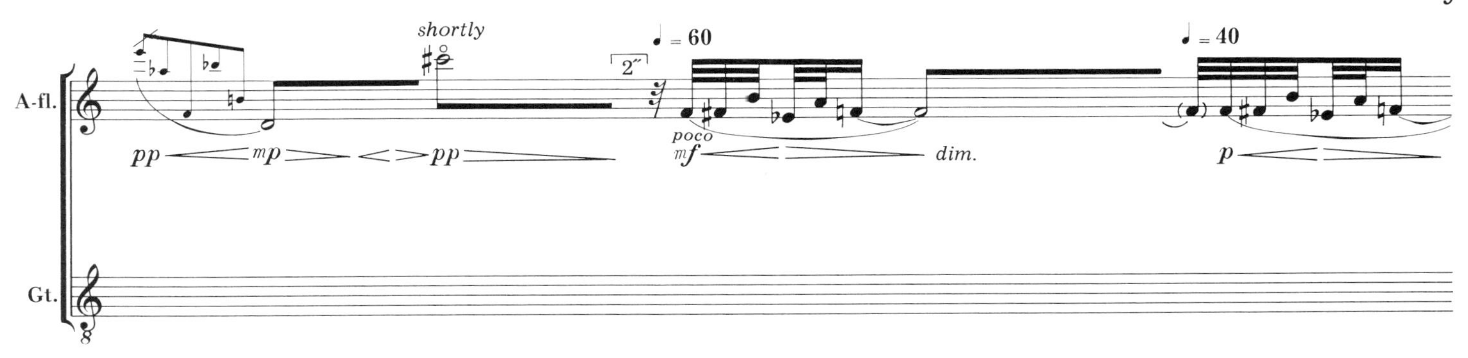
A-fl.
Gt.
shortly
2"
♩ = 60
♩ = 40
pp
mp
pp
poco
mf
dim.
p

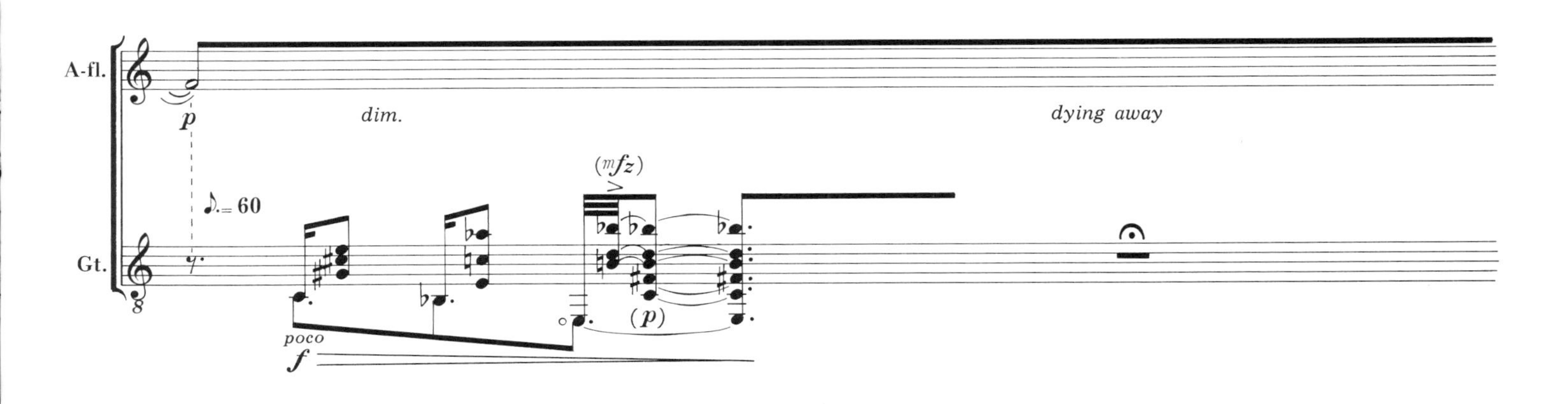
A-fl.
Gt.
p
dim.
dying away
♪. = 60
(mfz)
(p)
poco
f

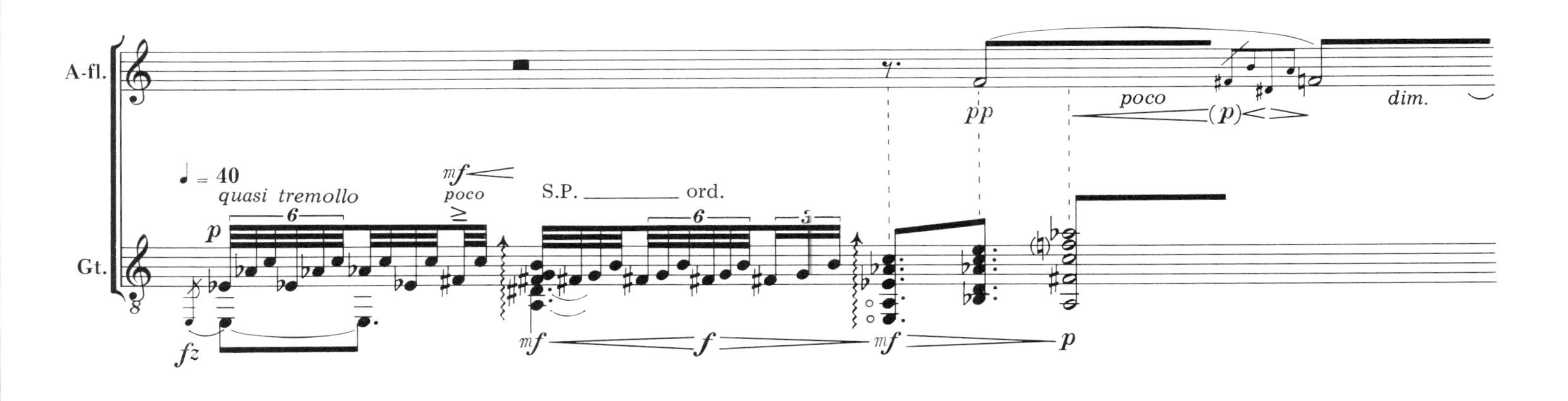
A-fl.
Gt.
♩ = 40
quasi tremollo
6
mf
poco
S.P.
ord.
6
5
fz
mf
f
mf
p
pp
poco
(p)
dim.

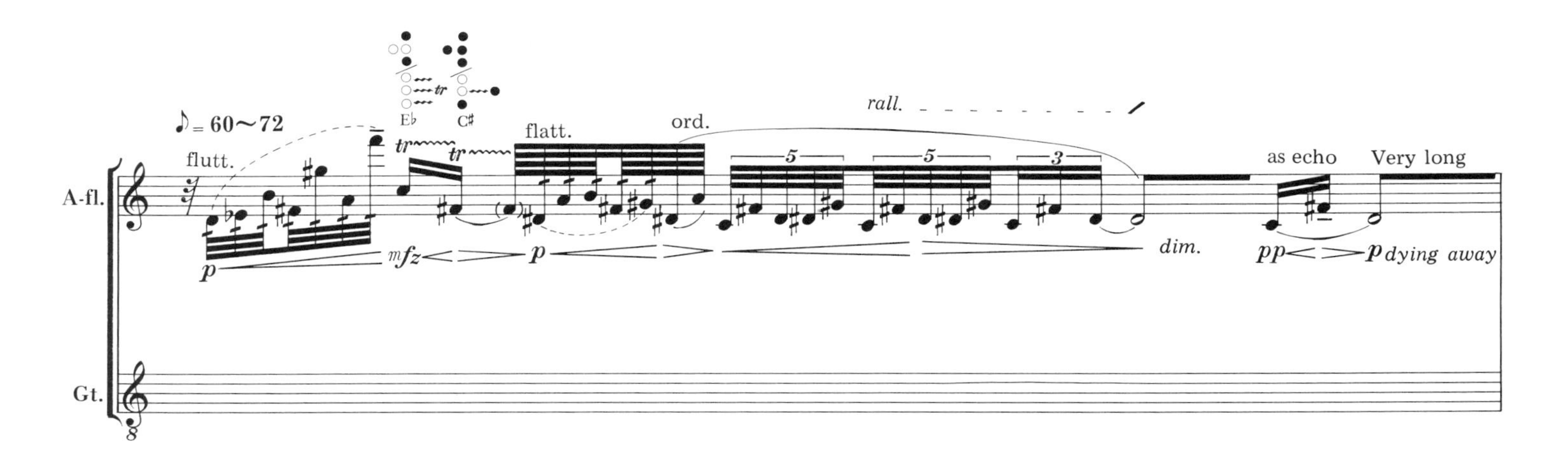
A-fl.
Gt.
♪ = 60~72
flutt.
tr
E♭
C♯
flatt.
ord.
rall.
5
5
3
as echo
Very long
p
mfz
p
dim.
pp
p dying away

A-fl.
Gt.
sub. pp
flutt.
mf
molto dim.
poco rall.
più mosso
♪.= 85~96
pp
mf
p
legato
tr
C♯
Normal
rit.
f
♪.= 85
2″~3″
♪.= 63
dying away
♪.= 40
♪.= 60~72
3/16
l.v.
damp.
3″~4″
pp
p dolce
poco
f
5

武満 徹《海へ》 ●

アルト・フルートとギターのための

初版発行――1982年2月27日

第4版第8刷⑭ ――2018年12月25日

発行――ショット・ミュージック株式会社

――東京都千代田区内神田1-10-1 平富ビル3階

――〒101-0047

――(03)6695-2450

――http://www.schottjapan.com

――ISBN 978-4-89066-307-1

――ISMN M-65001-044-3

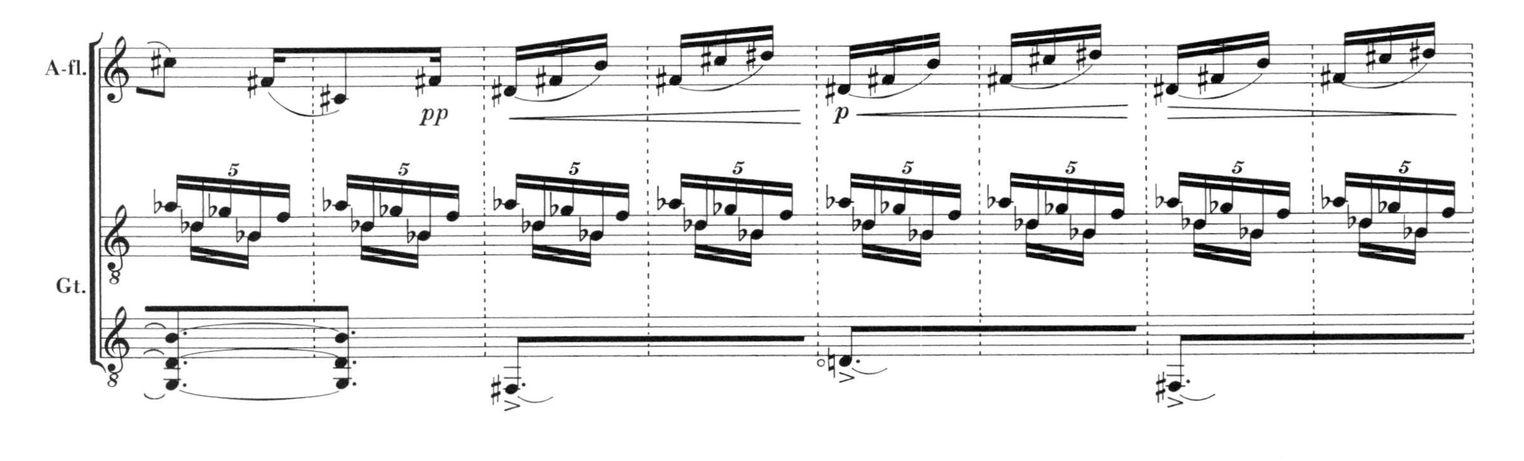
A-fl.
Gt.
pp
p

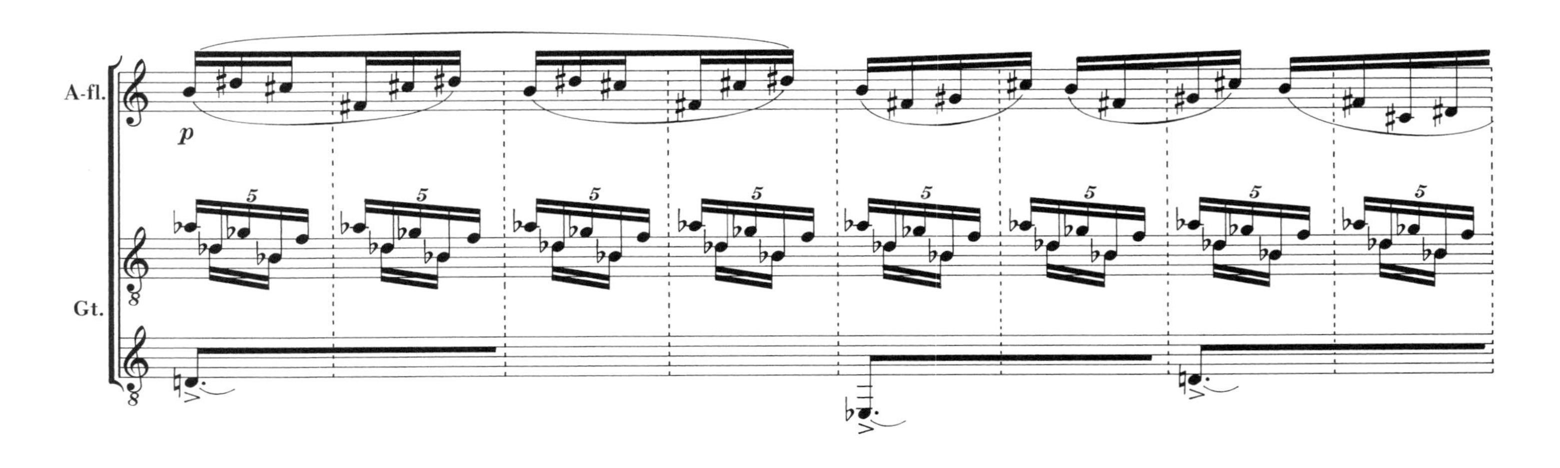
A-fl.
Gt.
p

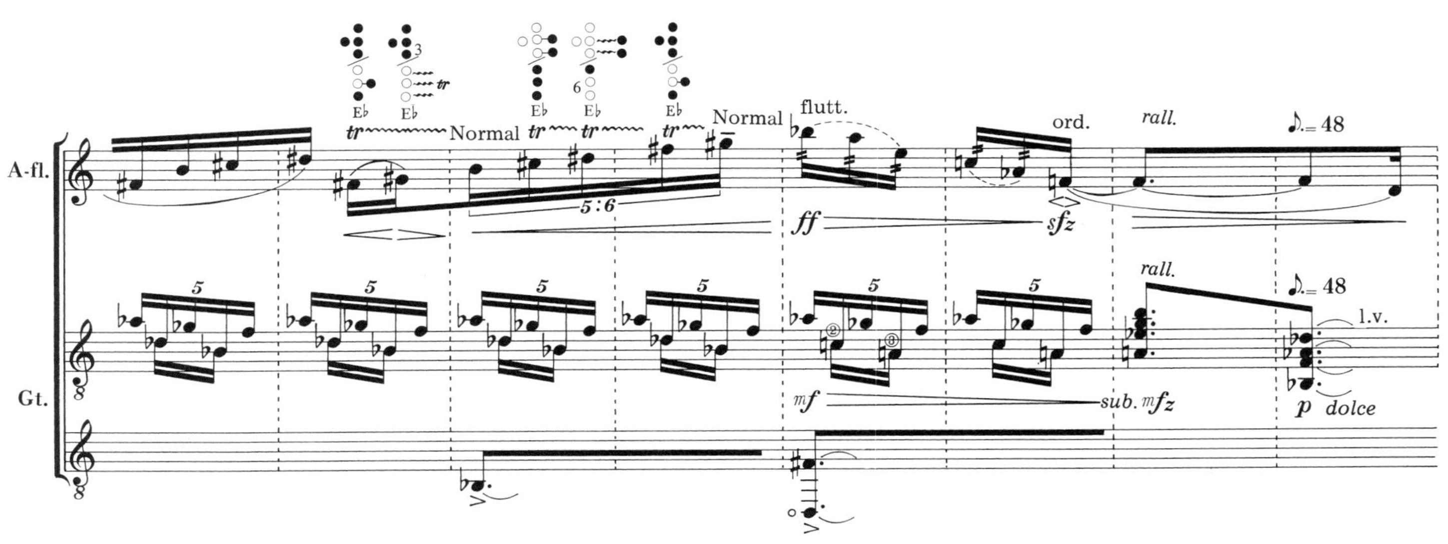
A-fl.
Gt.
Eb
tr
Normal
5 : 6
flutt.
ff
ord.
sfz
rall.
♪= 48
mf
sub. mfz
l.v.
p dolce

A-fl.
Gt.
flutt.
4 : 3
Normal
p
sub. f
sub. p
mf
pp dolce

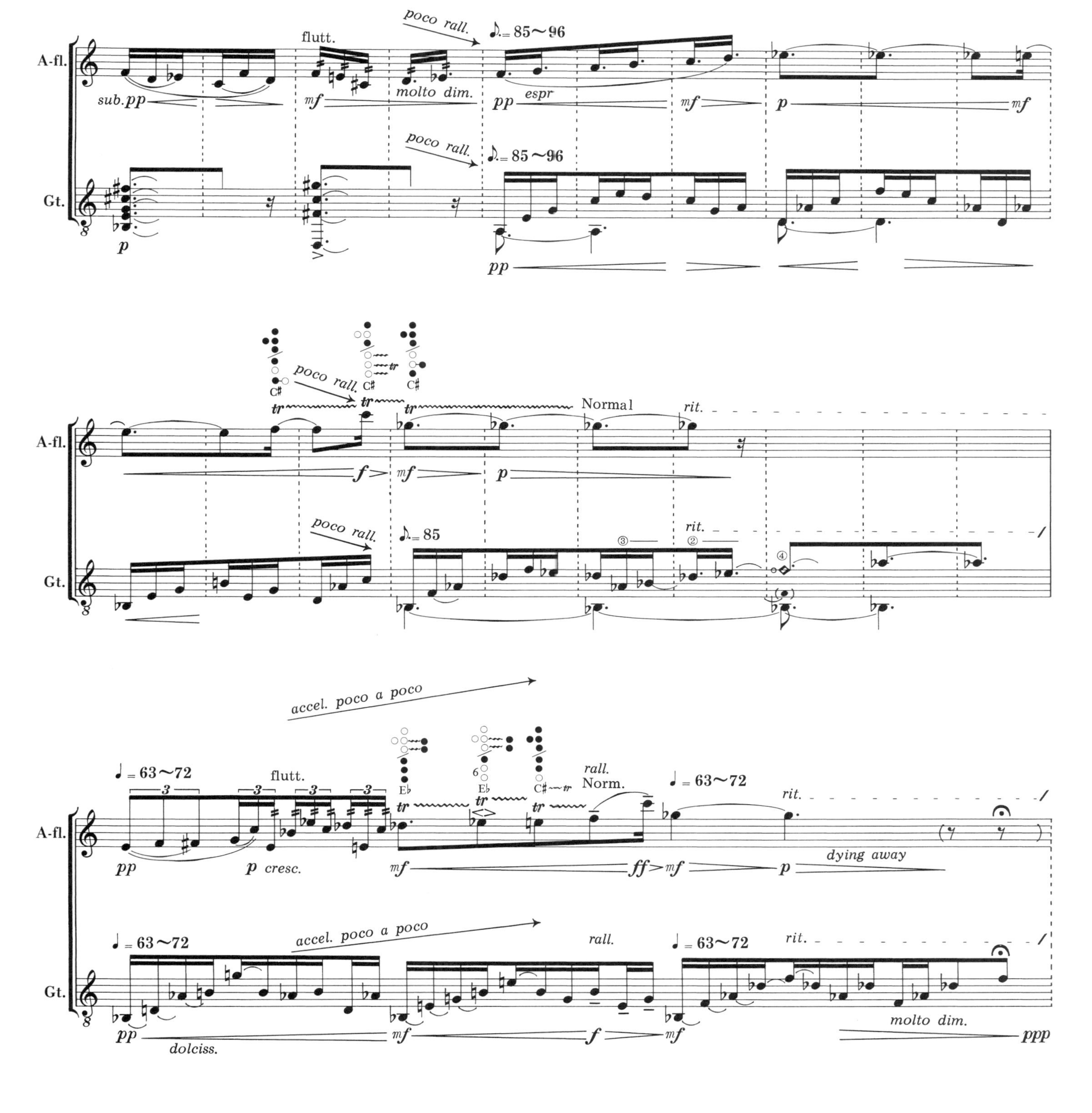
A-fl.
Gt.
sub.pp
flutt.
mf
molto dim.
poco rall.
♪= 85~96
pp
espr
p
poco rall.
Normal
rit.
f
♪= 85
accel. poco a poco
♩= 63~72
flutt.
Eb
C#
rall.
Norm.
ff
dying away
p cresc.
dolciss.
molto dim.
ppp

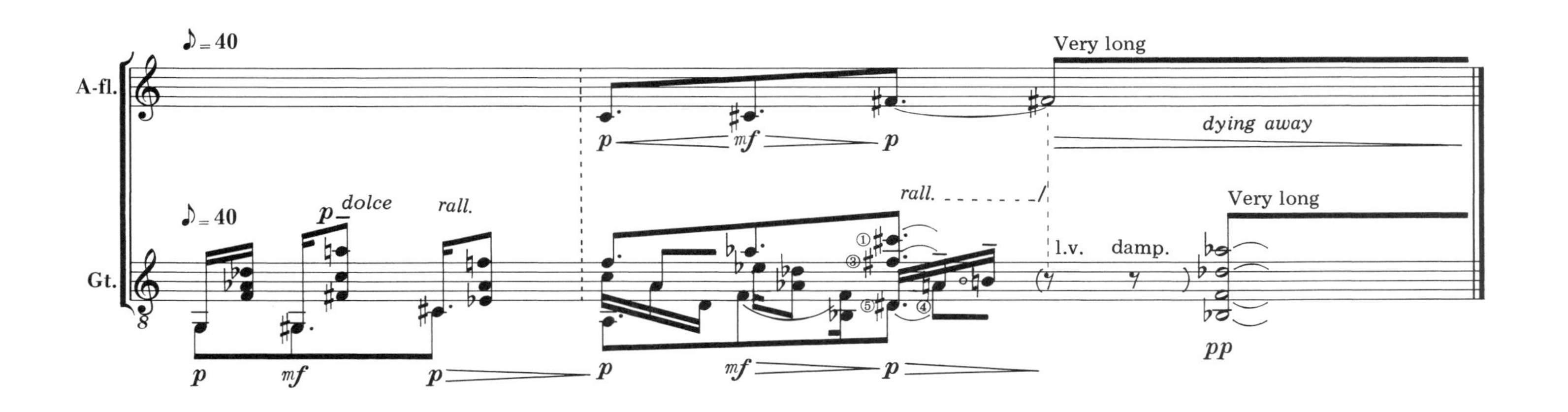
♪= 40
Very long
dying away
p
mf
dolce
rall.
l.v.
damp.
pp